My Bible Dot-to-Dot
In the Beginning

Retold by Christina Goodings
Illustrated by Emanuela Carletti

Choose crayons to match each group of dots.
Follow the numbers to draw a line from dot to dot.
When your picture is complete, add the correct
word sticker.

LION
CHILDREN'S

The world is just beginning. What is shining in the sky?

What's that tall plant?

Who has Long Legs?

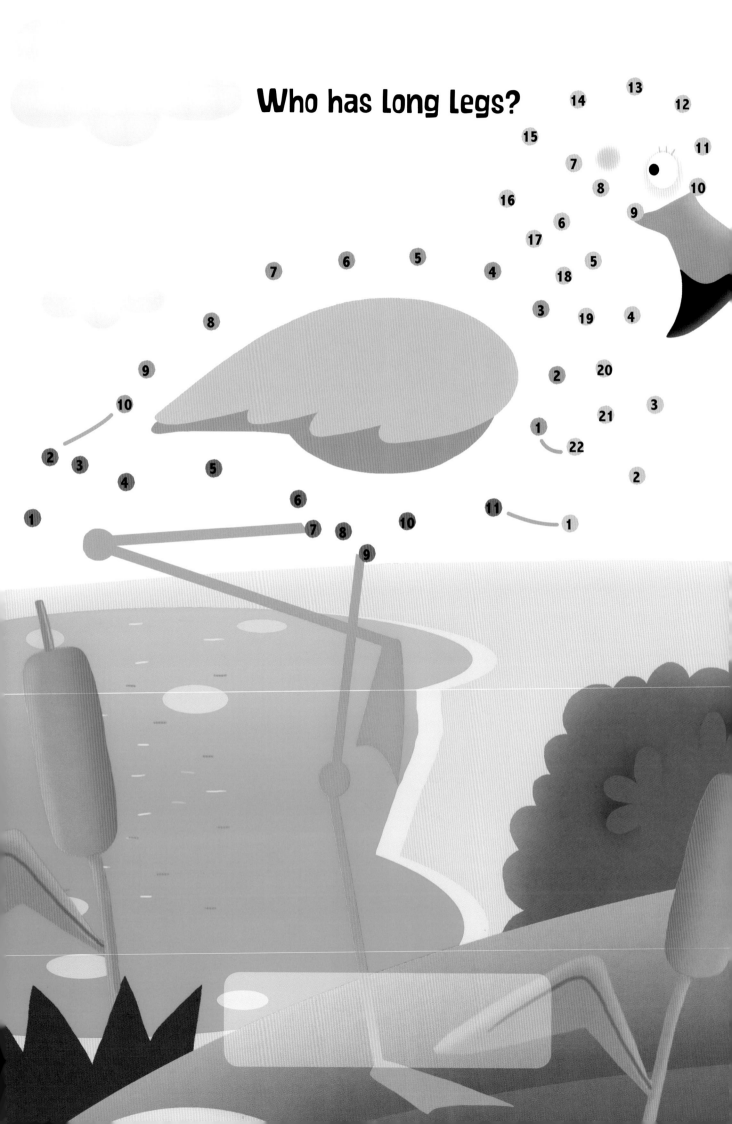

Who has a big beak and big claws?

Who has a big bright eye?

Who has sharp teeth?

Who has two horns?

Answers to pages

sun

palm tree

flamingo

owl

fish

shark

rhino

leopard

tiger

donkey

cow

sheep

Adam

Eve

dog

Who has spotty fur?

Who has stripy fur?

Who has long ears?

Who has a swishy tail?

Who is munching flowers in the meadow?

Who is listening to the birds?

Who is picking flowers?

Everyone's sleeping late. Who is snoring?